Jerrie's Journey

Jerrie's Journey

Jerald Hightower

© 2015 by Jerald Hightower
All rights reserved.

ISBN: 1514692023
ISBN 13: 9781514692028
Library of Congress Control Number: 2015910343
CreateSpace Independent Publishing Platform
North Charleston, South Carolina

To my two sons:
Ronald Hightower
Victor Hightower

To my mother; my deceased son, Steven Hightower; and the memory of my sisters; and to millions of others like them who dared to act on their dreams

Contents

Autobiography xi
Poems 1
    Break Every Chain 3
    Loving Him 4
    Living in the City of Memphis, Tennessee 5
    Racing for Time 6
    Creation of the Almighty 7
    Life in the Water 8
    Emotions 9
    Freedom Reign 10
    Sho' Glad I Am Free 11
    Storms on the Raging Sea of Life 12
    Sitting under a Cool Shade Tree in the Midst of Sky-Blue Water 13
    Beale-Street Poet 14
    Beale Street 15
    Beale Street, Blues Street 16
    Lost in Time 17
    Loneliness in the Midst of Time 18
    Mind over Matter 19
    Black Stone Rangers 20
    Country Girl Called Lillie Mae 21
    There 22
    Body and Mind 23

Stories 25
　　It's Not Too Late to Dream 27
　　Run, Sister Girl 29
　　I Had a Dream 30
　　Dream Team 32

Autobiography

I was born in Memphis, Tennessee. I grew up in a Christian home. I have five sisters. My mother was a homemaker, and my father worked for the railroad. At the age of fourteen, I began to sneak out of the house, always seeking older men because I was very pretty, with a great figure—110 pounds soaking wet. I was cute. I was dating older men in the neighborhood, and I would try to make it home beforefour in the morning, which was the time when my mother would wake up. One night when I was coming home aroundfour, my mother caught me coming in the window. I will never forget that night. She whipped me with a large switch hard until I told her that I was dead. As I lay there holding my breath, she hauled off and hit me as hard as she could. I was terrified.

Then I screamed, "I ain't dead!"

She had to stop whipping me because she started to laugh loudly.

My wildness had just begun. When I was in the ninth grade, I was dating a white man who was around twenty-nine years old. His name was Carlton. He was a bus driver. Now, this was during Jim Crow segregation between blacks and whites. I would ride his bus all day, and when he took breaks, I would go to his house with him. I guess we had jungle fever, as they used to call it back in the day. The amazing part was that he used to let me sit in the front seat with him, and he dared any one of the white supremacists to say a word. He would tell them, "She's with me." One hot summer night, he asked me to meet him to go for a ride. I told my mother I was going to a friend's house for a little while.

At around seven o'clock, we rode to a place called President Island. As we were having sex, lo and behold, we saw the police coming. We were so frightened. He asked me to get out of the car and hide, and he said he would come back to get me. I was terrified. The only thing that saved me was the fact that I was surrounded by tall bushes and lots of tall grass. I lay down on the grass, and I could see the police talking to him. I trusted him. About fifteen minutes later, they left, and he returned. I was one happy soul. When I got home, at about eleven thirty, I learned that my mother had called the police because she was so worried about me. When I walked in, she canceled the police call. I was home safe. Can you imagine how relieved I was after all I had been through that night? I never saw that man again. We thought it was too risky to keep dating, so that was the end of that story.

When I was fifteen, I was attending Booker T. Washington High School. I was practicing to become a majorette in the band. One day, I was late coming home from band practice. My band instructor, Mr. David, raped me and then told me I was too dark to become a majorette. I did not report the rape because I was not a virgin in any way, shape, form, or fashion. Satan had my coat.

While I was still at Booker T. Washington High School, I met George Hightower, who was on his way into a restaurant next door to the school. George later became my husband. He was twenty-seven years old. I was sixteen at the time. He was handsome. He was driving a 1954 black-and-white Chevrolet convertible. I was happy to get that ride that hot summer day. To make a long story short, he got me pregnant, we got married, and I never got a chance to go to my school prom, nor did I get a chance to graduate from high school. Years later, in 1964, I graduated from night school. Praise God.

At the age of sixteen, I was separated from my husband because of jealousy and physical abuse and went back home to live with my mother. I thought I was a grown woman, and I continued to date older men. I met a truck driver named J. W. Owen. He was giving me twenty-five dollars a week, good money in 1955. He was giving me money for food. I did not want to be tied down anymore. I was enjoying my freedom.

At age seventeen I went back to my husband, and he moved me to Mississippi to keep a close eye on me. I then became pregnant with my second child. I have to admit that I was not at all faithful to that marriage. I was so fine looking, like Beyoncé—fine body and shape. I had it all, and the men would not leave me alone. Honestly, I loved the attention. My husband used to abuse me badly. One day, he beat me so badly that I bled profusely from my head. I was admitted to the hospital, and they asked me who the president was to see if I was coherent. My third son was born a couple of months after this incident. I was happy to be back in what I called "the city," Memphis, Tennessee. My husband continued to abuse me. He did not trust me at all.

I went to visit my mom while he was at work one day, and I thought I had beaten him home this particular evening. When I got home, the lights were off, so I thought I had it made. Man, I opened the door, and he was there, drunk. He beat the shit out of me, in the dark, with a belt, and I was pleading for my life. I left him again and moved back home with Mom. This time, I got a job working downtown as a waitress and a carhop. It was fun, and I really enjoyed having my freedom. I decided to give my husband one last try at this marriage, but it did not work because he continued to not trust me and continued the beatings. By this time I was twenty-seven years old. The last time he abused and beat me, I had to be hospitalized again. This was the last and final blow, and I was done. I thought, *This man is eventually going to kill me.* Even though I was screaming loudly, the neighbors evidently could not hear me.

Finally, after living single, I turned twenty-eight. I began to date again, and I met the man of my dreams at a nightclub, the Hitching Post, where I worked as a waitress. He was about thirty-two. His name was Anthony. After three or four months, we moved to North Memphis so that my husband could not find us. I got a good job as an assistant dietician at William Bold Hospital, making good money. For eight years my husband could not find me. Finally, he saw me in South Memphis one day and followed me home. He had a confrontation with my new lover, who was taking care of me and my three children. After that, my lover's friend told him he was moving to California and asked him if he would like to go with him and his lady. I saw a chance of a lifetime that I was not going to miss out on. My lover asked me if I wanted to go with him, and I said yes. I took a two-week vacation from my job and left my sister in charge of my boys.

The rest is history—I never returned until this day! California has been my home now for fifty years.

I can still remember that amazing day when I left Memphis, Tennessee, with the love of my life. I was the happiest woman in the world and knew my life would change forever. On the journey to California with my lover, our first stop was this amazing city, New Orleans, filled with bright lights and excitement. Our next stop was Houston, Texas. It was bigger than Memphis and had more restaurants. Our next stop was Colorado Springs, where we stayed for two months with friends. I remember this place called Georgia Pizza that had beer, wine, and dancing. I made a new friend there, a white girl who use to call me "Sister Girl." We used to hang out every night, having fun. I began to see my life changing. I felt free from bondage and from living in fear. Our next stop was Los Angeles, California—Hollywood. Hot doggie! I thought I had died and gone to heaven. Bright lights, big city. I felt, lived, and looked like a movie star for one year. We lived with old friends from our hometown, Memphis. They made us feel welcome and fed us like we were royalty.

Our last stop was San Francisco, California, where we settled down and made our home. San Francisco was so beautiful; it looked like pictures I had seen of cities in Europe, like Paris and Rome. There were tall buildings and Victorian-style apartments, all close together. Tall buildings were nestled among rolling hills. I had never seen anything like it in my entire life. As a great doctor friend of mine once said, "Before you die, come to San Francisco before you go to heaven."

My first job was at a bowling alley in the downtown Tenderloin district, across the street from the hotel where we were staying. I worked as a cocktail waitress and made a lot of tips every night. My second job was as a carhop and cocktail waitress at Fisherman's Wharf. I made a lot of tips there, too. Finally, I made enough money to rent an apartment. My lover and I separated after eight months because of infidelity. I was so happy to live in an apartment instead of in a hotel. I felt like a big shot. For the next year, I worked in a small restaurant two blocks from my apartment as a waitress. Finally, I started going to school to become a nurse's aide and began to work in many nursing homes. However, I got tired of being a nurse's aide and wanted more out of life. I needed a professional job.

So I went to school to be a licensed vocational nurse. When I graduated, I began working through various nursing agencies. I made good money and bought myself a new car every two years. I got tired of working out of nursing agencies and applied at Kaiser Hospital. After I was hired at Kaiser, I went back to Memphis to get my sons. I worked there for thirty years and retired. What a wonderful career I had, meeting lifelong friends. At that time I was raising my three boys by myself. My sons had great manners and were obedient; they never got into any trouble with the law. Praise God, and thank you, Jesus.

God answered all my prayers. That's why today I am still praising my Lord and savior, Jesus Christ. He called me into his glorious ministry. I have been running for Jesus ever since, and I am not tired yet. Thank God for Jesus. I am still preaching the Gospel on the KEST radio station in the beautiful city of San Francisco, California. I teach a Bible study every Wednesday night, and I am preaching the Gospel of Jesus Christ in a church without walls, as Jesus Christ gives me instructions. Glory to the most high God. When he calls me, I will answer. I will be somewhere listening for my name. Love is the answer to our life's journey in this world that we humans live in. God bless you all.

Poems

Break Every Chain

Holy, holy, holy is the Lord God of hosts. In his name we rest.
The whole earth is full of his glory. He turns our pain to gain.
Darkness of our life is sin. Humility is to trust God's light.
God is perfect in all his ways. Approaching him is called humility.
Grace is filled with love and gratitude, the way he reaches out to us.

Loving Him

The black man on the railroad train.
He told her to meet him at the train.
He said, "Baby, don't be late."
Well, she got there late.
Waited at the gate, same train, same old game.

Living in the City of Memphis, Tennessee

Riding downtown,
saw rivers of water,
wishing I had my mate,
but I said, I still have life.
Well, it's never too late.
While looking over the seashore,
saw a boat, two men fishing,
heard the old songwriter singing—
let's go fishing.

Racing for Time

Looking in his eyes,
knew where the sun shines,
knew my place—
just had to run this race.

Creation of the Almighty

Riding downtown in Memphis, Tennessee,
Saw the river tides rolling back and forth.
Looking over the seashore, saw a boat,
Saw men fishing. Sister Girl strolling on the beach
meditating on God's beauty. Soft wind blowing, thinking
on the nature of the almighty creation.

Life in the Water

Riding downtown, saw rivers of water,
wishing I had my mate.

But I said, "I still have life."
Well, it's never too late. While looking over the seashore,

saw a boat, two men fishing. I heard the old songwriter singing, "Let's go fishing." I found my mate at the dock of the bay. Now I finally know how
to fish. Thank God.

Emotions

Are strong feelings love, hate, anger?
Or are they an Egyptian myth?
Slave's belief:
"The Sun God" and "Chief Deity."

Tail is our hind, bottom, inferior, fully dressed men—"just a slang."

T noun are the, those, and them letter of English alphabet. T was chiefly in poetry T 'was/the them and those. The people in Memphis. Those people in the street. Those people in the California show ain't the same.

Freedom Reign

Living in the fields of Mississippi, chopping cotton, didn't know much about history of black freedom.
Now I know from experience as a witness, we are all equal if we keep the mindset that we are all creatures of this universe. Manifestation from "our black ancestors was not to indemnify our roots." Let black freedom reign.

Sho' Glad I Am Free

Sho' found out I ain't no nigger.
Sho' glad I am free.

Sho' glad trouble doesn't last always.
Sho' glad God has set me free.

God done trouble the water.

Hallelujah, hallelujah, hallelujah! As Martin Luther stated,

"Thank you, God Almighty, I am free at last."

Black sisters and brothers, sho' glad trouble doesn't last always.
God done trouble the water.
Not nigger, but black and proud, black pride—sho' glad I am free.

Storms on the Raging Sea of Life

Storms raging the sea!

Rivers are the giver.

Moon is soon to show sun.

Shining stars looking through the mask,

seeing glass that fits the task,

meditating on time.

Sitting under a Cool Shade Tree in the Midst of Sky-Blue Water

Meditating on time,
Racing against time.
After graduating from nursing school, I worked at Kaiser Hospital for thirty years.
Retired 2000. I became very sick and was diagnosed with cirrhosis of the liver.
Soon almighty God answered my prayer, and soon after, I received a liver
and kidney transplant
and a five-way-bypass heart surgery.
I stood on faith. Psalm 118:17 says,
"I shall live and not die and declare the works of the Lord." Today I am
teaching and preaching the Gospel, "The Spoken Word," on KEST radio at 1450.
Meditating on time.

Beale-Street Poet

Beale Street!
Blues Street!
Found life stepping on my feet.
Found the gate! Found my mate, too.
Beale Street once was black.
Now it's white.
Reserve a space now safe.

Beale Street

Come to
Beale Street. Party here.
Party over there. Party everywhere.
Black Street. "Come and eat."
Blues so sweet.
Lots of booze blues clubs:
Bobby Blue Bland, B. B. King.
You will find life stepping on your feet.

Beale Street, Blues Street

B. B. King and Bobby Bland
were black, now are white.
Found life stepping on my feet.
Went through the gate, did not find my mate.
Same game show isn't the same.

Lost in Time

A man without a dream is lost in time, is hopeless.
Time is love.
Time suffers loss. Time is patience.
How long must we wait for a sign?
Time is essence to a dream.
Goals, must we be patient! Be love.
Charity conquers
all—wait on your time.

Loneliness in the Midst of Time

Realizing it's never too late,
he was at the gate.

Racing for time.
God only knows our time.

He will keep us in our right mind.

Only pray we want go back in time.
We still have our sight. Where is Mr. Right?

Mind over Matter

Blessed are those who walk in righteousness.
Mind over matter.

Don't scatter the mess—it's the best
mostly for the poor who trust the test.

Almighty will survive in the midst of time.
Where storms arise, he will shine.

Rice, ice, bugs, thugs—same ol' game.
You know my name.

Living on the seashore,
tell me once he will tell you twice.
Eating rice for survival, living on ice,
walking down Memory Lane—it's just
mind over matter of time…

Black Stone Rangers

There they are,

thirty at the corner.

Black, raw, and ready.

Sores in the city.

They do not want to heal.

Country Girl Called Lillie Mae

Hi, there. My name is Lillie Mae. I came to California from Mississippi.

My girlfriend said that I was so country. She said I could eat fried ice cream.

I did not know what she meant until six months later.

In Mississippi we were not taught what fried ice cream was!

Well, I told Sister Girl my name ain't Sally Raspberry, and I don't eat fried ice cream.

Only to find out later that it meant that you are stupid or dumb.
My name is Lillie Mae!

Living in California, found out twenty years later there is a restaurant in San Francisco

that sells fried ice cream.

Lillie Mae! Not country at all. Ha! Ha!

There

In the beauty of holiness, doves are here, Holy Spirit there.
Eagles flying here, birds singing in the air, praising God everywhere.
Ships in the sea, on bending knee, saints are there praising God everywhere.
Servants of God there. Debra, I know you are there. I can hear you saying,
"Look to the hills."
Where cometh your help? Your help is coming from the Lord Christ Jesus.

Body and Mind

According to my belief system and the way I was raised in the South,
it was more important to enslave your body than to enslave your mind.
To enslave your mind is the belief in the brainwashing effects of one's behavior
and belief.
One's mind includes body, mind, soul, spirit,and actions. Again, belief, behavior
thought to the way it sounds.
"West Africa" recorded via James Weldon Johnson's

"Reclamation." Ebonics, our language lost centuries ago. Spirituality is more important to enslave someone's mind plus action. Most importantly, a slave master's goal was to enslave one's body and one's mind. However, enslaving our mind was not the birth concept of black pride, knowledge, and freedom as a nation.

Mind, memory is to bring to mind a story; opinion is to speak your mind, thinking, feeling, sanity, paying attention, being careful of not being offensive to others. Our intention is to be concerned, watchful, paying attention to one's feelings—not to neglect, ignore. Mind is the psychological behavior to recall memory, consciousness in thinking to pay attention, to be obedient to rules of behavior.

A body, a person, a human being, physical substance of a human being or animal or plant. Nature is 70 percent water. Human being, body language, body movements, same as nonverbal communication. Human body has shape, frame, dust, ashes, body, soul, spirit. "Body and soul stay alive, earn a living to survive."A body is a physical, human organism, again with form, figure, frame, shape. Anatomy, bones, guts. We are a group of individuals, society, party, bodies, and souls together.

"Master, you can whip me all day, but you cannot enslave my mind."

Conclusion: Body reacts with mind, soul, and spirit. Without a body, we are likefidels, robots, birds flying in context.

Thank God! He gave us our minds.

Stories

It's Not Too Late to Dream

Once upon a time, there was a girl named Sister Girl.

Sister Girl was so country. Back in the day, she ate fried ice cream. They called her "Gofer." She would go for anything, so she got fried.

During Jim Crow segregation, when she worked for the white minstrel, the white men all fell in love with her. Sister Girl was so fine; she was shaped like a Coca-Cola bottle. That girl would ride the bus line with her white minstrel all day and sat in the front seat with him. He dared anyone to say anything. He knew he would soon do the nasty.

Well, soon Sister Girl got tired of playing the same old game. Soon she fried that old minstrel solider and dared him to say that they had been first at the end of the line.

Sister Girl was so fine. Sister Girl did not take no mess. She had her way with men; she would always have the last word. She got married at sixteen years old and had three children. Her husband would beat her badly. She got tired of being abused by her husband, so Sister Girl soon divorced him.

She left that old town called Memphis, Tennessee, with her lover, who wined and dined Sister Girl and treated her like she was a princess. They traveled to Colorado Springs, Denver, Houston, and Mexico, and then they finally arrived in Los Angeles, California.

Sister Girl arrived in California only to find out her lover was a player. She soon hit the streets for survival. She met a movie-star producer, who cast *Tarzan & Jane*. He desired her but was smart and knew it was only a game.

Conclusion: Sister Girl fired her lover. She ran off and met a girlfriend, went to nursing school, graduated, worked at Kaiser Hospital for thirty years, and retired. She is presently attending Merritt College for her business degree. She would like to give thanks to her instructors, Professor Hodari Davis, Professor Hillary Altman, Counselor Peggy Jerome, and finally, Professor F. Mofidi, for encouraging her and telling her that it is never too late. Thanks also to Dr. Adams, president of Merritt Community College, for his inspirational speech he gave at Acts Full Gospel Church that it is never too late to dream of one's goal and to return to school and complete one's education.

Run, Sister Girl

Racing for it, looking in his eyes, knowing where the sun rises! Knew your place, just had to run this race. "Run, run, Sister Girl."

Racing for time! Looking at time, my experience a rhyme! Thomas Jefferson notes on the state of virginal America, first-race writing:

"The need for African-centered analysis, philosophy, afrocentricity, cultural perspective, African culture, and behavior context and statute was based on experience."

Father of black history, Carter G. Woodson, states, "To handicap a student by teaching him that his black face is a curse and that his struggle to change his condition is hopeless is the worst sort of lynching." I have learned in this class that in 1933, this miseducation of the famous Negro father of black history is the way to control his way of thinking.

Paul Robinson, old man river, singing on a boat about freedom. Ra! Egypt myth, the sun god and chief deity God symbol radias. Ra! The eighteen[th] letter of the English alphabet, ta! The nineteenth letter of the Greek alphabet, group of languages spoken. Utterance, line on line. Tacitus silent.

Writing poetry inspiration, immediate feelings, emotion, metaphors, telling the story. To hear how they sound, to slow freely and naturally. Imagery eloquent ideas open lines five to ten lines experience. Feedback positive or negative from critics, from audience.

Ideas, expression, love, feelings, motions, signature. Life story. Impression, autobiography, life adventures. Reaction in response, spoken words, sermons. Muhammad, Muslim true believer, Islam to resign oneself to God, Jewish scripture, Christian.

I Had a Dream

I, Jeraldine Hightower, in my sound mind, would like to ask my sons, Ronald Hightower and Victor Hightower, to forgive me for leaving them in Memphis, Tennessee. I want you to know that I never stopped loving you and missing you. The reason I could not take you guys with me is that I was not financially able at that time. I was looking for a better life for us. I love you, Ron and Victor.

When I saw my chance at a better life for us, I took advantage of it. I had no money. George Hunt had a friend who was visiting him from Los Angeles, California, who needed a way back home and got a ride with a white girl. He asked George if he was ready to leave Memphis, and George asked me if I was ready to leave Memphis.

I had a dream a long time ago to leave Memphis—a long time ago—when a long-time friend showed me a picture of California. I thought California looked like a place where I would like to live. And my friend, Lavern Stuart, had moved to Oakland, California, to a navy base. I thought, *At least I know someone who lives there in case we get stuck out there.* When she used to come visit in Memphis, she used to tell me how beautiful California was and how beautiful the weather was, and all those things came to my mind. That helped me make up my mind to say, "OK, this is my chance, and I will never get this chance again to leave Memphis."

Ronald, I want to thank God for your love and patience, because I know you had a dream and that you prayed every day. How God answered your prayer! I thank God for you, too, Victor. You have always been a worker. You love to work and have gained extensive knowledge by going to college and graduating from three schools. Thank God for how he has blessed our family. I thank God for you guys not giving up on your mother, who loves you dearly—more than I could ever express. I was a young mother who had to learn how to be a good mother as a teenager, pregnant with my first child at age fifteen.

Thank God for Mrs. Bessie Coleman, my mother, and Carolyn Grear, who helped me raise you guys. You know you had the best God, who was also watching over you guys. That's why I love him so much—because his eye is always on the sparrow, so it is written.

Dream Team

In closing this book on my experiences in life and my expectations, it would not be fair to close without giving God his glory and thanksgiving. First, I thank God for the miracle that he gave me in October 2005—I was blessed with a liver and kidney transplant. Second, I had a five-way-bypass heart surgery, also in 2005.

I was diagnosed with cirrhosis of the liver in 1997. At that time, I was a party girl, drinking alcohol and not eating healthy foods. Being a nurse who worked the late shift, I would leave work and head for the bar with my coworkers. I became very sick at work one day and passed out on the floor while giving medication to my patients and was rushed to the emergency room. I passed out again at a friend's house and was rushed to the emergency room for an ectopic pregnancy. I had emergency surgery and received a transfusion with five pints of contaminated blood, from which I contracted hepatitis C.

I want to thank my three sons for standing by my side while in transition for the four months I was in the intensive-care unit awaiting the liver transplant. I also want to thank my two sisters Carolyn and Jean for being there from Memphis, Tennessee. And I thank my in-home caregiver, Ms. Jannet, who was also a blessing to me. Let me tell you, I was so sick until I thought, *If I can make it through this terrible nightmare, I will be a walking, living miracle.* Thank God I made it with what I call the "dream team," my doctors at CPMC in San Francisco.

I know now, in 2015, looking back on my history, that I am a walking, living miracle. I am now taking a miracle medication called Harvoni, which is called a wonder drug. It is 98 percent effective. I am seventy-seven years old but look like I am fifty and not a day older. My peers notice that I am well kempt and well-groomed. In giving glory to the almighty, I am preaching on the radio every other Sunday morning, giving God praise and thanksgiving. Also, I am teaching a Bible study at the senior-citizens' center on Wednesday evenings, trying to give back to God's people a token of thanksgiving.

I am truly grateful and thankful for my healing. And now, as a retired nurse, I'm enjoying my life riding the BART (Bay Area Rapid Transit) bus, not walking with a cane, and making all my doctors appointments—sometimes with my son and sometimes with my caregiver. God has set me free and allowed me to live free, not in bondage. Thank God almighty. I'm free at last from liver disease.

Made in United States
Orlando, FL
01 December 2023